RAC
Journal

RAC
Journal

One Adventurous Girl's Firsthand
Experience of the Tough but Rewarding
Annual Ride Across California

KAILYN DONNELLY

Published by Inspire Books
www.inspire-books.com

Paperback ISBN: 978-1-950685-30-1
Ebook ISBN: 978-1-950685-31-8

*A percent of the proceeds from this book will go to
the Ride Across California volunteers.*

Acknowledgments

To Mike and Denis, the founders of RAC. Thank you for starting this amazing opportunity thirty years ago and continuing to uphold it. I think it's amazing you two are still riding and giving support to the riders, parents, volunteers, and chase teams. RAC has without a doubt impacted my life beyond words, as I'm sure it's done for many kids who couldn't be more grateful for your encouragement and passion. Thank you to Denis for all of the inspiring pep talks and goosebump-raising stores, and to Mike for your helpful, positive attitude and assisting everyone as needed on the training rides. I couldn't have done this without you two!

And thank you, of course, to my parents! From the get-go, they were right behind me, nodding along with my spontaneous switch to do RAC. They always pushed my to do my best but allowed me to take a break when I needed. A special thank you to my dad, who completed Ride Across California with me and knew my struggles firsthand. Thank you both for your endless support in writing this book and sticking with me throughout this journey.

Contents

Preface

The day started like any other; school, right up until when the clock's hands finally read two. The bell's ring exploded through the halls as Mrs. Regardie, my teacher, smiled "Have a great day!" at the students shoving each other out the door. She had no idea! I rushed over to one of my best friends, Jessica. This afternoon we were going to hang out, and I couldn't wait!

"I'm so excited for tonight!" Her chocolate brown eyes sparkle with happiness.

"Same!" I agree as we head for the cafeteria, where we congregate for sign-in for the after-school program, chatting about all the crafts and games we'd play once we were picked up.

***

"So girls, do you have anything special planned?" Mrs. Leibowitz, Jessica's mom, asked as we sat down for another one of her delicious dinners. Jessica and I spiral into conversation, stumbling over each other and then backing out to let the other answer.

"Oh yeah!" My eyes light up. "I'm getting a new bike soon!"

"That's cool." Both mother and daughter look happy for me.

"But I don't really like bike riding, and on top of that I can barely ride over any hill, no matter how small," I say.

"Then why get a new bike?" Mrs. Leibowitz brings to light what my young mind had skipped over.

"Huh—I guess I didn't really think about that." Really, I had always had a bike in case we went camping or there was an occasion to use it. It never occured to me not to get a bike as soon as I grew out of my old one.

"You should do RAC," Jessica says, looking at me.

"I—I don't know," I shrug at the unanticipated suggestion. Jessica's fate was already sealed, as her older brother had done it three years before, and she wanted me to tag along with her and Coral, who was also following in her brother's footsteps, so she could have two friends to talk to. They continue on to tell me how enriching it would be, and that this would be my only chance to seize the once-in-a-lifetime experience. I had long ago ruled that I wasn't going to leap out of my comfort zone, but I stopped to reconsider. They did make it sound really fun and gainful, and I knew I wouldn't be able to regret not going.

That one bit of reconsideration changed my life.

Intro

*All About the Six Months of Training
I Completed Preparing for RAC*

I throw my arm wildly behind me, flinging the nozzle of my Camelbak to my open mouth and guzzling a mouthful of the lukewarm water I had poured in the morning that seemed so long ago. My legs ached with every pump of the pedals, and my arms sagged beneath my handlebars, limp with fatigue. My unsteady front tire crests the tip of the hill that appears so much shorter than it actually is, my calves screaming with relief. I pull into a parking lot just left of where we came to a stop near a shopping center, bundles of kids and their parents slowing to a stop to walk their bikes to their car. My dad and I praise those around us and each other with another ride well done, and start the way back to our truck. I check the clock adjacent to the radio on the dash (the one that's always eleven minutes ahead), and glance at the time: 2:54. Late, but just enough time left in the Sunday to wrap up my homework and pick up my room before retiring to bed.

Now imagine this, but once every week. If you're considering RAC, you probably know, or at least assume, that you don't just show up at the starting point and tough it through all the elongated hills and long, hot hours. The minimum requirement of miles total 350, and the recommended time to get a-going on this would be around the beginning of October or end of September. And while that may seem like a hefty load, you can count on the RAC team to unfailingly ensure there's an available training ride every weekend, unless there are complications like weather. It indisputably assists those families with parents who are busy with work, or you and your siblings, and don't necessarily have the free time to map out the trails, times, and distances for an outing every week—while still checking that it suits the guidelines of the adventure you've decided to undertake. Furthermore, they help you ease into being comfortable riding with a large group, learning the ways of the road, and shifting and getting on and off your bike. Other than that, the only ride that's mandatory is the Escondido ride, which you have to complete twice. I would for sure say that ride was one of the most arduous, but it's also one of the ones you can be most proud of. And they don't put you through these challenges for fun—it's always to make sure you are ready to take on RAC and can have the best time while doing it. Along with that, they do hold a couple meetings to just talk about RAC and what you do in more detail, the best supplies to bring, what type of bike you should buy, etc.

My favorite ride had to be the one we did in celebration of the winter holidays. If you wanted to, many people strung colorful lights around their bikes. This was the only RAC ride we did in the dark, but the security was amped up so no one got hurt. We were also riding along the 56, where there is a bike path that's wide and fenced off from traffic. It's the one ride you end up repeating a bunch, probably because of its accessibility and beginner-friendly difficulty level, so you get to know it pretty well. After the ride, you chow down at a potluck! The variety of food is delicious, and you can linger to talk to all your friends. Definitely not one to miss!

Day Zero

April 7, 2018

Five-and-a-half months leading up to one week, and that one week that was going to commence tomorrow. As in less than twenty-four hours! Tomorrow is Ride Across California (RAC for short), and I'm out-of-this-world ecstatic but unsurprisingly extremely nervous! It's 7:09 p.m., and Dad promised we'd take a short trip to Vons after the football game (he's currently engrossed downstairs—I can hear his outbursts of disapproval and relief from up here!) to rush a quick raid for snacks. The RAC leaders do provide a wide variety of goodies and refreshments, most of which is water or Gatorade, but it's good to be prepared for when you're alone or not riding. When we get back, I plan to jump into the shower, get our name tags for our bikes ready, and settle in for the night. I'm still slightly sick and sore from the Jog-a-Thon yesterday, and I'm pleading it fades before we head off tomorrow. The Jog-a-Thon is exactly what it sounds like: every year, my elementary school holds a Wellness Day, a day dedicated to learning about health, and part of it is to run, or jog, as many laps as you can in the limited amount of time given.

Back to my day, I gobbled down a protein-rich break-fast, roamed around throwing odds and ends into my plastic storage bucket (we didn't use suitcases or duffle bags), and filling up the idle time getting more and more anxious. On an unrelated note, I just downloaded three new games, so I also played on those. After an uneventful but seemingly packed morning, I changed, slipped on my raggedy knee pads, threw my long, light brown hair into a modest pony-tail, and slammed the door to my mom's car, who was going to deliver me to my volleyball game.

Makenzie, one of my closest friends who also happens to enjoy the amazing hobby that is volleyball, was playing on the other side of the double court gym. We're the Cherry Bombs, seeing as we have red jerseys, and my team was composed of Vanessa, Kera, Franky, Bailey, Fisa, Hanah, Kelly, Alexis, and, obviously, myself. Coach Rod, Coach Chad, and Coach Rod's daughter, who we all considered our enthusiastic cheerleader, were waiting for our team to congregate at our bench. I met up with my team and, after an uplifting pep talk, we circled our hands and raised them with a shout, a grin on all of our faces. In case you didn't know, one volleyball game is split into three sets, and which-ever team takes the majority of the sets triumphs. Following the exhausting but totally worth-it game, I high-fived all of my teammates as well as the opposing side and then headed home, where I continued skipping around with my dad getting ready for tomorrow.

And that's where I am now. I'm so nervous! I know I already mentioned that, but imagine having to present an hour-long speech memorized in front of a stadium of people. Multiply that by ten and you'd have yourself a pretty accurate idea of what I was feeling. Oh, and double that in anticipation mixed with eagerness and thrill. But at least I'm undertaking it with good friends: Jessica, Coral, Soraya, Maddie, and Alexie. That was essentially my day, and because I have nothing more to say on the subject I think I'll start getting ready for bed. Bye!

Day One

RIVER TO GOLD
ROCK RANCH

April 8, 2018

I'm here, sitting alone in my dad's old, blue truck trying to not go ballistic because of this really annoying beeping sound. I have no idea what it is and everyone else is outside—I'm just camping in here because I have nothing to do and, when presented the choice, would sit over stand. Even though it's getting rather hot. Whew, the sound went away. Finally! I remembered a lot of things to pack this morning that I had forgotten last night, so hopefully that means I'm not forgetting anything. Also, this is going to sound weird and off-topic, but it smells strongly of cologne and I have no inkling as to why.

To recap, I woke up at 7:10 and started to finish packing, in the process saving myself from having to buy things later, as I mentioned earlier. When we were ready, we dropped off our things at the Penske (a big yellow truck the leaders rent to transport our things in), which was parked next to the library next to our house, so we luckily didn't have to drive far. On the way we spotted Soraya and Maddie, both who happen to be classmates as well as friends of mine. Next we went to Golden Bagel and Starbucks for breakfast. We headed back home, and my mom braided my hair in long plaits. I like to do this when camping or going on a trip, so I don't have to worry about brushing/taking care of a thick mess and so it doesn't get in my way.

My plan was to write in the journal (which I'm doing right now), and sleep on the two-hour drive to the starting point of the RAC at Yuma, Arizona. We're supposed to depart at 10:00, and we're thinking about picking up some In-n-Out for lunch on the way there as many others did, jumping on the bandwagon. My other plan was to shower Tuesday, Thursday, and Saturday. I'll rebraid my hair by myself on Tuesday, but because Mom and Gavin, my younger brother by two years, are visiting on Thursday, my mom can braid my hair then. As you can see, I have many plans, being the *very* productive and responsible person I am. I'm going to Gordon's, my friend Mckenna's dad's, birthday party on Saturday, but I'm gonna be super tired so we'll play it by ear to see if I'm up to partying. I'd also be guaranteed late if I do end up going. That's all-see you later!

*Did I mention the whole "theme" of RAC is "River to Riptide," as in the Colorado River to Moonlight Beach? Sorry if I already have or it comes up again.

~Later, before bed~

I'm waiting for Jessica to stop by to go to the bathroom to brush our teeth. Campfire starts at nine, so we have time. Dinner was pulled pork in a bun with corn on the cob and baked potatoes. It was okay, but this campground isn't the best. But first, let me start from the beginning. Waves of families arrived at the starting point, gathering all their odds and ends and hugging their goodbyes. The point is that you dip your back tire in the Colorado River and your front tire in the ocean. River to Riptide.** My dad and I walked down to wait in line with Soraya and her dad. In the process of posing for the picture, I misstepped and my foot sank into the squishy mud, coating my shoe in a thick, rocky film-not a good time. When I said goodbye to my mom, it was melancholy thinking about how I was going to miss her.

My dad and I dipping our tires in the Colorado River

Then we were leaving! I was near shaking with nerves, my thoughts rushing and fleeting. I watched this video about bees this one time, and instead of stinging a wasp to protect its hive, a bunch of bees will surround the wasp and flap their wings to create enough body heat to burn the wasp to death. An accurate visual of my stomach, long past the point of gentle butterflies.

Not even a fourth of a mile into the trip we hit a sand-bank, and are forced to pull our bikes beside us. I'm predicting right now that this may end up as one of the worst parts, and I'm probably right. It was beyond humid and stifling, waves of heat rippling along the horizon, and we were dragging our 100-pound bikes through thick sand. Dust kept clogging my socks, which instantaneously started to feel crusty dusty (my phrase for unbearable). We were constantly pausing to catch a breath and sip of water warm from the heat, slowing our pace and making it more difficult to continue each time we had to stand back up again.

On one of the stops, I brought out my Vaseline. Dad stuck his finger in it to use some, but his finger went straight through—it was pure liquid! Oh, it was so hilarious (I know-it's one of those you-had-to-be-there moments). But no joke, that part was *hard*. At the onset of the turn back onto asphalt, we were able to laboriously pedal to a chase stop close by. A chase driver is someone who has a car and parks at the side of the road for anyone to take a quick break or fill up on water. We met Alexie, but when we left it was

Jessica, Mrs. Leibowitz (Jessica's mom), my dad, and I. We were riding on this almost abandoned road off to the side of the freeway and the road was *super* bumpy, which for me makes all the difference. So you can just imagine I was having a grand time!

At one stop we let my Dad go ahead because he was faster and we didn't want to slow him down. Once we started along a road, I was cruising leisurely, the soft breeze whispering past with a sigh of content. Somehow or another, I got ahead of Jessica and caught up with Dad. We stopped to take a picture of the sunset—it was so pretty! Splashes of bumblebee yellow and powder blue seeped into the horizon, the sun a big ball of flaming light suspended in pure clarity above the silhouetted cacti. I made a pact right then and there that I'm going to do that every night. Just cause I think that'd be cool. For the rest of the day, that stretch of road was the only we were going to see, before we turned off onto a dirt path to the campsite, a haven nestled away from traffic. The times before that I was riding solitary before I caught up with Dad was nice, just to be able to think thoughts without any real purpose. We turned left onto a slightly sandy and very bumpy road. I was literally getting a headache from the bumps. When we turned onto the road, we rode into the sunset. The sun actually didn't bother me much. I might've been dirty and sweaty, but I felt like a metaphor-like princess riding into the sunset (used a simile to describe a metaphor). That sounds kinda lame, but you know how the main hero or heroine, like, rides into the sunset at the end of every story? Kinda like that.

Pause: Right now I just heard this random kid say, "K, *Mom* got the comfortable bed." And then the dad shushed him. Oh, how funny. Anyways, I finally saw the Penske—hallelujah. The Penske means victory! Because, you know, that's where all our stuff is, so it's either camp or a break, either of which would appeal to me at any time. I couldn't find Jessica's dad's immaculate white Chase truck (meh grumble grumble), so my dad proposed we start to set up our tent behind a creepy metal shack. Ah, no! You should've seen the thing! We compromised by moving a smidge away from the rusted metal. It was frustratingly annoying because he kept coming up with actually good points like, "We're not crowded around other people" or, "The ground is smooth—see, no rocks!" which made it really hard to argue with. "But it's creepy!" I reasoned. That may seem wimpy, but I don't really care what you think because it *was* creepy. And I did relent. We set up, found Jessica, and had dinner.

Gotta say, this camp isn't really my favorite. But spooky things are fun, especially when you have Denis sharing a ghost story around a flickering campfire, casting light on faces that were otherwise shrouded in shadow. Apparently, Denis, one of the two founders, the other one being Mike, always has a pep talk and story to share around a campfire. There wasn't always a campfire, but that was the coined title, with a capital *C*. After Jessica and I headed to the bathroom, Soraya joined us and we hung out until campfire. The introduction included some background history about the campground and gold mining, I think it was. And no, it was not boring at all. In fact, I found it terribly interesting. I think I'll even take some pictures along the trail.

I still can't believe I'm doing this, and I'll never certainly never forget it (says the person writing in a journal)! It's impossible to fathom, even without my smoothie of emotions, dreading but also anticipating and eager for the remainder of the week. Don't get me wrong, I'm glad I'm doing this; I'll just be half glad when it concludes. Alright, well, time for me to hit the hay.

**Not even a paragraph later . . . tsk, tsk, tsk. Well anyways, I'm too lazy to delete what I repeated, so deal.

Day Two

GOLD ROCK RANCH—PINE VALLEY SCHOOL

April 9, 2018

Morning! Last night I had a surprisingly good sleep, but I'm a tad bit disoriented and groggy. Last night it was uncomfortably warm, but I was so tired I fell asleep almost right away. For me at least, waking up at 6:00 isn't too bad, since that's what I normally do, but today all I wanted to do was sleep in. I'd write more, but I have to hurry and pack my things!

~That Night~

I'm back! I thought I was tired yesterday, but it's nothing compared to today. I could collapse on my sleeping bag right now, but I'm trying to write down everything so I won't forget it. That is the only reason I'm not passed out snoring (I don't snore, by the way, I just meant, because you know, I'd be sleeping). Anyways, after I packed up and dropped everything off at the Penske, I had breakfast with Soraya and our dads. I gobbled down half of a toasted bagel with peanut butter and jelly (not together, separate), some hard-boiled eggs, sausages, and a delicious handful of strawberries. Plus some baked potatoes. Over the course of the RAC, I picked up that you eat even when you're not hungry to store enough calories to complete each day. I hummed with nervous energy for the upcoming take off, especially since Monday is the longest of all the days with fifty-four miles, but I was ready.

We left on the same bumpy dirt road that we'd come in on, and eventually we hit an asphalt road. Last night the route turned off the road onto a dirt path, but this morning we backtracked where we left off and continued on in the opposite direction. I didn't get two feet when I was struck with unbearable heat and raging winds, making the few hills that were monstrous in incline and length even more challenging. To make matters worse, the wind was headwind, and not just normal headwind. It was fast and strong, and with every minute I found myself desperately wanting to reach snack.

On the other hand, it was gorgeous, but focusing on every turn of the wheels made all the glances I caught of the landscape fleeting. I'd also never been one to risk riding without holding onto the handlebars or looking away for too long. When we started at 8:00, the sun was rising above the impressive purple mountains, creating a storybook sunrise. They rose to my right, or the east. The mountains reminded me of the square cloth that had been pinched in the middle and pulled skyward.

Finally, I could make out the striking bright yellow Penske parked in a vacant, bland dirt lot. I rode in, thankful to have made it to the anticipated rest. Their filling snacks helped boost my energy levels and mood, and I had some free time to chat with my friends and peers. When the time came, we proceeded to cross, or more accurately scramble, across the road onto the bike path, smoothing into a line. For the next portion, because it consisted of more downhill than uphill, it was required that everyone rode in groups of four; three others to constantly check your speed on the sloping terrain and to add strength in numbers against the oncoming vehicles. I left with my dad, Coral, and her dad, Eric. The rest of the way was no problem, mainly because the downhills propelled us up the uphills, so we skipped labor almost entirely. After an abundance of ups and downs, we hit lunch.

Lunch was held at this old-fashioned shop constructed of raw wood with benches that would give you splinters if you weren't careful, and whose shop sold faded t-shirts and tacky souvenirs, and even gave you change in two-dollar bills. We silenced our rumbling stomachs on picnic tables under the shaded entrance. I had a PB&J and a cheese stick, which I'm normally not a fan of. After a satisfying lunch we started off, and passed beautiful sand dunes that rolled with tranquil slopes, smooth and warmed by the beating sun. I heard someone say that on some of them they had filmed Return of the Jedi!

While riding a long, gradual hill, I noticed how the sand dunes rose high on either side of us. It was such a serene feeling, completely surrounded by tan sand that had probably been there for thousands of years, constantly eroding and building. After the endless hill, we bumped along on rocky asphalt. Everywhere I looked I saw sand, but this time it was flat and bushes were settled interestingly neat. They added a pop of moss-green to the scenery, resting in rows and columns. I also can't forget the huge gust of wind carrying sheets of sand that blinded me and almost knocked me off the hill! We rode for what seemed like forever. People kept telling us different miles and we were hopeful and discouraged many, many times. We turned left and Bam! Snack!

When we left, I tried to sneak to the front so I could get a good campsite, and I succeeded. We rode through farms, which was a really good change from the dry desert. One part had an exotic palm tree farm on my right, which was nice, don't get me wrong, but I was just so tired flat roads felt like uphill, and I could only focus on getting to camp. I couldn't wait to relax on the dewy grass and stare up at the robins egg blue sky slowly fading to twilight, pinpoints of light streaking through the endless veil of darkness.

Moo! I turned my head and saw a huge pen of cows! They were so adorable. At that point we turned right, and it started to smell like gardening gone wrong. Stupid cows. A river, more a man-made irrigation tunnel, ran in the opposite direction parallel to us. All of a sudden, we were at the school. I was shell-shocked because it was only 1:40, and yesterday my dad and I hit camp after 5:00 with a significantly less mile count. Maybe it had to do with when we started, or how long it took to drag our bikes through the dense sand.

We were in the first chunk of riders to finish, and Dad and I were lucky enough to get an awesome campsite for the second time in a row. Dinner were these out-of-this-world cheesy potatoes and hot dogs. Jessica, Coral, and I put our artistic skills to the test decorating Jessica's dad's car windows with these special markers made for the smooth surface. It turned out great, and I had a blast laughing with my friends while we filled in blocky letters with neon dots and lines. This is actually a common practice in the RAC community; many families fill their windows with motivational phrases, checkpoints of the journey, or just colorful patterns with the words "Ride Across California". By the time we were finished, stars were starting to twinkle into view and mostly everyone was settled or settling into the tents peppered across the yard.

Wow, this day flew by! Speaking of, it was time for the meeting. I rushed over, excitedly waiting for yet another chiller but instead receiving something even better: an inspiring pep talk that temporarily made me forget every hardship, melting away to leave only the victories. While I couldn't recite the whole thing from my patchy memory, his speech consisted first of telling us how well we did on the longest day, adding in some stories of kindness he found particularly warming, and then motivating us with his past experiences on previous rides and reminding us that it's really all just one step at a time, and that before you know it, you'll be at the camp you'd been longing for all day. Even faster will come the day you'll be riding onto Moonlight Beach on Saturday, the last day. Where he shared his wisdom, he also set out a docket for the week, and that's when I learned that tomorrow we'd be riding over a plate boundary. How cool is that? Well okay, maybe it's not as awesome as dinosaurs coming to life along the trail, but it's at least a little interesting.

I bet you that without RAC, I'd never think about the concept, much less do it. My mom sent me an encouraging quote via Mrs. Leibowitz: "Maybe strength is what you have left when you've used all your weak." Hmm. Hadn't thought of it that way, but good point! Unfortunately I don't know who said that. Wait. No, I couldn't find it, but here's another: "I am strong because I've been weak. I am fearless because I've been afraid. I am wise because I've been foolish."-Unknown.

Did I forget to mention I love this campsite? It's so nice, with a stretching grass field and playground. The only thing is that they don't have drinkable water. I couldn't imagine going to school knowing I couldn't drink any water there! Oh yeah, I just remembered we have to wake up at 5:00 and leave at 6:30, because school is still in session. I honestly can't believe I'm doing this. It all seems so surreal, even after it's started! Hopefully the rest of this week is enjoyable and not tremendously difficult. Alright, I'm about to collapse, it took all of me to stay up and write this, so goodnight! P.S., the stars are gorgeous! Probably as pretty as in Mammoth (I would definitely recommend visiting!)

Day Three

PINE VALLEY SCHOOL TO OCOTILLO

April 10, 2018

It's currently late at night. I'm not sure about the time, I just know it's late. Whew, today was hard. I actually loved the morning, it was windy but in a relaxing and calming way, and you got to ride through the sun rising. It was after the pool (lunch), that I didn't like. In the morning, I was super cold and didn't want to unwrap from my sleeping bag cocoon, but I finally forced myself to get ready. Yesterday morning I was fine, but this morning the extra hour of sleep was missed. The plan was to go swimming at lunchtime, and you had to put your swimsuit and towel in a separate bag because you weren't going to be able to access the Penske later. So I did, and headed over to gobble down breakfast. It consisted of egg bake, cereal, and hot cocoa. There was something else but I can't remember. Coral eventually showed up and we sat together. When I returned to our tent, I found out my dad had packed my swim bag and it was already in the Penske. It sucked, but I could have told him in advance. Plus, there was nothing to be done. I rolled my bike over to Jessica, and we left.

Anyways, when we left, it was chilly, but a good kind of chilly. I was wearing my new red-orange jacket, which, by the way, I totally urge you to look into. It's just like a paper thin jacket that keeps you warm, but that also blocks the heat, meaning you can wear it all the time. Anyways, Jessica and I were just cruising along. Or we were until the roads turned mercilessly rocky and uneven. Fortunately, Jessica—bless her—thought to ride on the white line bordering the road. Oh, it was a dream-contrastingly smooth.

We were riding through more farmland, by the way, and we saw a small group of black cows, but not in a pen like last time. I mean, there was a fence encompassing the field, but it was open and more spacious. Apparently we rode next to alfalfa, or so my dad said. He had trouble deciding whether it was alfalfa or barley, both some type of plant. Oh yeah, we also rolled by purple cabbage (heh, look at me, thinking you care what type of plant I rode next to).

Lastly, we saw some super-cute goats, their fur a scratchy

coffee-creamer brown. We eventually got to the base, where the pool was. Part of me thought the base was super cool and that the pool added an extra something to the trip (plus, like, being cool on a hot day), but the other half was thinking that it took time out of the day and might've added miles. Like, the mile count would have been less if we didn't take a detour to the pool. But it added some variety to the week and was something different. Prior to that excursion, we regrouped at like this park with small water jets and stuff, and where Mrs. Perkio bought me a swimsuit. I couldn't express my gratitude at their generosity! Lunch was a turkey and cheese sandwich, an orange slice, sour cream and onion Pringles, and a Capri-sun. To be allowed into the deep end, which was most of the pool, you had to pass a test administered by a lifeguard. Coral passed, but the minimal effort the evaluation took didn't pique Jessica's or my interest. But after wading in the quarter of the pool we were given, Jessica and I succumbed to trying it out.

At the base for lunch and swimming

Right as we were in line, Christiane, one of the main leaders, came out with an announcement. We had two options, but they came with a condition. One, we could stay longer, (yay), or you could leave right then. The thing was that we'd have tailwinds or no wind until four o'clock, and then it would switch to headwinds. The logical option would be to leave, because then you would have as big a chance as allowed to make it to camp before four, which is what we did. Because we're logical.

Alright, I'm back. I had to tape my bucket—you know, my substitute for a duffel bag—lid because it cracked. So, um, yeah, the fact that winds would start later got all of us out of the pool. But after the announcement, I got to do the test. You had to swim across the pool (I did freestyle) then tread. Jessica and I both passed. I did a jump off the diving board and swam to get out. Right as I was pushing myself off the edge, Coral pointed out I had a bloody nose. I guess I didn't notice because I thought the blood was water. But don't worry, none of it got in the pool. Blah, I hate having bloody noses. I hurried to the bathroom, and this super nice mom helped me. Jessica and Coral showed up for moral support too. Uh, it was such a dramatic experience *dabs tears.* I just don't know how I survived. So not related to the story, there were like these kids playing and then they decided it was time to hit the hay. Before they left, I rested my head on the bucket to take a break from writing, and the mom asked me if I had a tent to sleep in. I told her I did. Isn't that so sweet? But, yeah, they left, so now I'm in peace and quiet. Ah, silence. Sometimes it's nice to be quiet every once and awhile.

So yeah, back to my day, I fixed my bloody nose, and we started on the road. Jessica and Mrs. Leibowitz left before us, but Coral stopped and I kept going. It was like 110 degrees and it *felt* like 110 degrees. Also the roads were really bumpy—no savior this time! Hills were a thing. We saw Plaster City, an old city with buildings that were used to make plaster for homes before plaster went out of style.

Right when we passed it, I got *another* bloody nose, which was great. It was super hard to keep going and find motivation, but eventually Dad and I caught up with Soraya and Phil, Soraya's dad. They were speeding along, making good time, so my goal was to keep up with her, but my dad had to stop. Soraya, being the nice person she is, waited with us but took off before we did. Oh, by the way, there was like no wind at all. Which was good, even though we were going to make it to the camp by four o'clock which is when the winds were scheduled to change direction. We rode a tiny bit more, down a big hill, which was everything! It felt so nice to finally relax.

The bridge to ride across was closed, so we had to walk our bikes through sand, and that was torture. Still stifling. On a positive note, fractured sunlight made the flecks of gold in the sand shimmer medallion, a sight to behold. Finally we made it to the top and back onto the road. We only had like five miles left! Soraya was well ahead of us, and so was Phil, but luckily I was still with my dad. Eventually

I ended up losing him, but met up with Phil, and so we got to ride together. Yee*

See, on the RAC everyone's friends and looking out for each other. You pass and meet up with other people as you're riding. Let me just say, it's practically impossible to stay with the same people the whole day. Everyone's positions are constantly changing. So you'll be riding and you turn around and whoops! You accidentally rode ahead of your friend. Or, you'll be like, "Oh hey! I remember you! Yeah, is it okay if I ride with you, I kinda lost everyone. Really? Well gee, thanks a bunch." On the RAC, there's no such thing as enemies. Except if that person took the last Goldfish, well then it's on.

Anyways, enough of my rant about how I learned so many life lessons that I'll probably use until I die (don't really know how learning that on a week-long bike trip you pass and meet up with tons of people is a life lesson, but whatever). We finally turned onto the road to camp. I'm telling you, those last three miles were the hardest. But I kept pushing myself, and I made it. Soraya was there to greet me, and my dad was originally behind me as mentioned before, but pedaled ahead to video me. I almost forgot to take a picture of Plaster City and the mountains. *Almost.* The inconsistent ombre mountains were breathtaking with the straight, clean white windmills positioned at their bases. The mountains were broken up with ridges that heighted with a deeper, richer shade of purple-violet. The mountain's imperfections poked and hid in different angles and drops, and it was so indescribably something out of a fairytale.

At camp Dad and I got a good spot again! Our luck is prevailing! Right next to Soraya, in shade, and on the playground. The only thing was that the street lamp was right above us. And it was going to be on. All night. I don't know about you, but I'm the kind of person that likes to sleep in complete darkness. Like, I can't do naps. Unless I'm super tired (obviously) or traveling. I hung out with Jessica and Coral the rest of the time and got my picture of the sunset. For dinner there was mashed potatoes, green beans, breadsticks, rolls, and brownies.

Also quite a funny dinner with my friends. Ok, last thing, well second** to last, but Coral and I heard a story about Christiane last night, about dogs and rats and some girl blurted out, "That's why her license plate said that!" Coral was curious if that was true, and so was I, so we looked for her car and asked people for help, and her license plate didn't have anything special on it. Finally we found Christiane herself, and she said it was the license plate on her *bike*. That was a wild goose (or rat?) chase for nothing! But I was bored, and that was an adventure that filled the time.

Lastly, we had a campfire. It was nice and I'm really excited for tomorrow because it sounds really easy and short. Today was forty-eight or forty-nine miles. Denis' story was good too. You know that constellation with the guy and the arrow? Achilles, I think? Every night it was visible, but tonight it's the most beautiful and lucid.

*Ok, so this is me editing, and I'm wondering why I just threw that in there. Like, um, hello? But it's staying.

**Again, I'm editing—yes, hello—and between writing

this and editing it, I tripped up in my grammar and thought those curious people out there would like to benefit from the knowledge. So for normal numbers, if the number is ten or under, you write it in letter form, and if it's eleven or greater, it's in number form. Same with ordinal numbers. Ordinal numbers being things like fourth, seventh, or twenty-second. Cardinal numbers are just normal numbers. Or, in Chicago Style, you spell out numbers one through ninety-nine, and everything else is written in number form.[1]

---

[1] This book obviously adheres to Chicago Style!

Day Four

OCOTILLO TO VALLECITO

(It's Wednesday, my dudes)

April 11, 2018

Right now Christaine is using spy music instead of a cowbell to wake us up, and I love it! I'm actually writing this on the morning of day five because last night I just couldn't. I woke up thirty or fifteen or twenty-minutes early (I don't even know anymore). Dad woke me up this morning, and I asked if the bells had rung yet. He said no, so he woke me up a whole, glorious six minutes early! I was annoyed because, like, a whole six minutes! But then the music started playing, so I guess it didn't matter. I got up and started to get ready. For breakfast I had a banana, milk, a hard-boiled egg, and I forgot the main course. I'll leave a space if I remember. Cheese sandwich (I remembered). Then I finished cleaning up. Today was twenty-seven miles. When we left, immediately I felt like I was carrying the sky on my legs (*cough, reference—kind of). They were so sore! Luckily, it wasn't too hot, but it sure was windy.

I started out with Coral and Jessica but at some point lost Coral. Alexie's mom was in front of me for a little bit, and she was super nice, helping and encouraging us. We had to go up hills, but they were workable, and then we hit the rest stop. Our path was winding through the mountains; there were mountains on our left and right and also ahead of us. We were heading west, so the sun was rising on our backs. The mountains were super pretty, and we got a few pictures. For snack, I had a good snack of Nutter Butter and gummies and I think a Z-Bar.

We had to leave in groups of six because we were going down really steep downhills. My group was Jessica, Mrs. Leibowitz, Coral, Eric, Dad, and I, and we left near the end. The downhill part was great, but it was really steep and a parent had to be stationed in the front and back and volunteers were there along the way to make sure we weren't going too fast. Also my hands started to hurt from just pumping the brakes the entire time. After enough time that even a downhill seemed like labor, we made it to the bottom of the hills. Eric got a jumping cactus stuck in his foot—but no need to worry, it was extracted. Then we continued forth, but it was just my dad and I and when he stopped he said to just keep going. When I passed a chase stop I caught a snippet of Hamilton, and I frowned; music was really what I needed, especially because it was Hamilton (I was obsessed with it back then).

It was getting noticeably harder, the heat and wind kicking it up a notch. As I glided along, I saw the unbelievable: the Hamilton guy. Yep, you heard that right folks, he caught up to me and was now blasting Washington On Your Side. And would you look at that—he had a name! Behold Otto, who will forever be in my good graces. But like seriously, he was super nice, asking if I liked his music, let me draft (when someone larger goes in front of someone smaller to block the wind), asked if we were riding at a manageable speed, and also if I needed to stop. It was then I glimpsed the Penske, settled in a little green bowl-like haven just chillin' in the completely barren, arid desert. I was overjoyed, and by that point Oliver, Otto's son and fellow Deer Canyon student, had caught up to us. When I entered camp I realized it was lunch *and* camp. I was surprised but relieved that the riding day was over. I was so tired! I had a PB&J and a banana.

I just heard the morning bell to wake up, but I need to finish writing so I'm just going to continue. So dad had got a campsite—again—next to Soraya, Maddie, and Alexie. Then I hung out and took my first shower of the week. I know, I know, I'm disgusted too. That's another thing too: RAC is not for those who need a shower like every night. There will not always be one available. When I released my mane from its braids, it poofed out in all directions, frizzy and curly. My shower which felt just *wonderful*—surprise, surprise. I was after Soraya and the water was still running, so I didn't have to use my quarters. I braided my hair in french braids for the first time without a mirror and they actually felt ok.

Dinner was breadsticks, steamed veggies (heh, when you're too lazy to write *vegetable*), pasta, and cookies. I got one oatmeal raisin. Yes, I do think they're good. I detest anyone who doesn't. So, everyone.

Before dinner, to pass the time, I played adult bingo with Jessica, Coral, Soraya, and Sean. It's where you put an adult's name under a category that applies to them. You know, those games you play with your class at the beginning of the year to get to know people. When the person running the game calls their name, if you have it, you cross it out. And then you get a bingo. We had to put the kids' names because there weren't any adult cards to draw. There were more rules too. I won a black dice, but I was the last one to win.

Jessica, Coral, and I had dinner in Coral's RV, and we yahooed around, laughing at things no one would find funny. Then we settled down, just chilling, when it was time for campfire. And tonight there was actual fire involved! I barely held together through it all, though. Not gonna lie, I'm nervous for tomorrow's ride, but like, more than usual. Tomorrow's the infamous "Banner Grade" (trust me-I didn't know it was a thing until RAC started either). Apparently it's just like the worst hill on RAC. Sounds fun. Oh, and it's supposed to be extra windy too. Can't say I don't believe them, wind has been slamming into me all evening. The story tonight was like about some ghost or something or other-it was so-so. It was such a short but long day (totally makes sense, right?). Got to go, but I did get a picture of the sunset that wasn't that colorful but still pretty!

Day Five

VALLECITO TO SPENCER VALLEY

April 12, 2018

A gain, I'm writing in the morning because I fell asleep watching TV, so I woke up early to finish writing and started getting ready. It was super hard to do anything because it was really windy. Like, windy beyond measure. At least it cooled my hot cocoa so I could drink it instantly. Then I had breakfast, which again I could barely hold onto. It consisted of Mini Wheats, but like in those tiny boxes, fruit, a small muffin, and a steak and egg burrito. And of course the hot cocoa mentioned earlier*. Then I hung out with Coral and got ready to ride.

On top of my usual nervousness, a lingering cloud of sadness hung over me as well. Last night Denis had said that that night and morning was the last time we'd all be together, because people were renting hotels tonight in Julian and sleeping at their homes tomorrow in Escondido. So I made sure to say thank you to all the people who helped me. Then we were off, and it went downhill from there. What I mean is, it all went uphill.

I rode with Jessica, Coral, and Alexie. At some point along the flat road we were going on we lost Alexie (yes, I know, I just said it went uphill, but there was a hill right in front of us, and, I mean, who starts on a hill?). When I started, I crossed the road and then turned left to start my journey. It was flat mostly, which was nice, but I really had to fight the wind to stay on the road. Following others behind and in front of me, I was literally being shoved over the pavement. We fought the wind with every ounce of our strengths, and suddenly the hill on the horizon was looming over us, shadowing our battles against the invisible. Right before we hit the incline, Jessica was blown over and fell, her handlebar hitting her head. She was OK, but didn't particularly want to continue in these heinous conditions. And I mean, who would? This was witnessed by Christiane, who allowed Jessica to stay with her. In that mess, Alexie and Coral got ahead of us. We, at this point it was just Mrs. Leibowitz and I, followed. Halfway up the incline, the largest gust I'd felt that day blew through, flinging Coral into the road and throwing her bike, which flew through the air, squashing her. Someone brought her to the side of the road, and we called for her dad who was behind. Coral was sniffling but seemed okay, and Eric stayed with her, so it was just Mrs. Leibowitz and I from there on. I decided I wanted to walk my bike just up and down the hill because of what happened to Coral with the wind. So we walked up the hill, and my dad was at the top directing traffic and helping people. The two of us pursued the decline, hopping back onto our bikes when it leveled out, still as windy as ever.

We passed this little shop with a driveway off the road, where Nicholas (an alumni) informed Mrs. Leibowitz that that was where Jessica was as well. We pulled into the driveway to see Jessica and just casually conversed, Soraya and Phil catching us as they rode by. After a short chunk of time, the four of us packed our bags and continued on. Phil and Soraya were faring well, and we didn't want to slow them down, so they rode on ahead. Along the route Mrs. Leibowitz and I happened to meet Eric, so we joined forces in fighting the merciless wind. Then, after the treacherous Box Canyon, we ran into my dad, who looked shocked to see us, as he had been relentlessly attempting to catch us, thinking we were ahead. There, boosts of tailwinds started to roll in, and it was swell. Turning a corner revealed a picturesque panorama of sloping slices of layered granite, the sinking sun hugging the horizon. Immediately the trail curved downhill, and we cruised through, soaking in all the hues and aromas. Along with the breathtaking scene, tailwinds gently nudged us forward. Time lapsed and suddenly we were pedaling into snack at an old, country-style convenience store that gave me vibes of dusty tumbleweeds, prickly, fern-green cacti, and coffee-brown horses rippling with strength and agility. It was announced that the rest of the ride was canceled, due to the wind, and that the plan was to carpool to our camps and hotels in Julian. They added they haven't seen wind like this in ten years, the strongest reaching speeds of up to sixty miles per hour!

From the compacted all-purpose store I decided to purchase a postcard (I'm a bit of a collector), hot cocoa for later, and Funyuns to munch on, and headed to Coral's RV to take a ride with her and Jessica. In juggling topics of conversation we rode, at one point right over Gorilla Hill, which was—no joke—straight up. They said that they were going to have a makeup ride for the ride that we were missing (Spoilers! I do it.). After we arrived at the pizza place (lunch), I was a little carsick from all the twists and turns, so I laid in the long grass, and it was super peaceful and comfortable. I swear, I get car sick so easily. Like, I can't read, play games, look down, any of it, because I'll get carsick. Despite that, I actually love car rides. And now I'm really off topic—moving on.

Then I played with Jessica and Coral and had lunch. It was a RAC tradition to end the day with Julian apple pie, and so I had that for that for the first time. It was delectable, and pies aren't really my thing, so that's saying something. I got the crumble and Coral and I shared an original, which was flaky. Then we went to the hotels, but my dad was getting stuff, so I went to Jessica's room and watched "The Middle" on TV. My mom and Gavin came and after we got everything in our hotel, we ate dinner at the pizza place. Lunch was pizza and bread rolls. Then I went back to my hotel and watched TV until I fell asleep. I also forgot to take a picture of the sunset! But I got the sunrise. Ugh, I was mad for forgetting but I couldn't really do anything about it, so I just shrugged it off. I think I'll do the makeup for today. I did thirteen of fourteen miles. Bye.

*Why do I think you'd care about my breakfast, or really my food at all? Well, unless you're considering RAC and decided to read this because you totally want to be convinced, and food is big to you. And I guess it is part of my day, and this is a journal about my day. So never mind. You *should* care.

Day Six

SPENCER VALLEY TO ARCHEOLOGICAL CENTER

April 13, 2018

O kay, it's actually April 13, I'm writing this at night. Today was probably my favorite. I woke up in the hotel, then I got ready. I guess I slept ok but I kept waking up because of dreams. Don't you just hate it when that happens?

Then I got ready to go to breakfast at the pizza place.

It was really good! Fruit, a roll, oatmeal with brown sugar, raisins, milk, scrambled eggs, and potatoes. Then we started getting ready to leave. When we left, it was a little windy. I was with Coral and Jessica, as usual.

Then we left and encompassing us were lush green valleys speckled with flowers from every side of the spectrum, and you could just feel the soft, gentle spring breeze dancin'* by, soothing you into a tranquil lull. We rode literally next to cows and, hey, they were so cute! Oh, their little noses! Then we hit a hill that reminded me of Escondido, one that was long, gradual, and a little steep.

We took a breath at the top and somewhere Jessica caught up to me, and Coral kept going. Then we rode on a neat dirt trail winding around mountains and under canopies of trees that had the light splashing through the leaves in playful splinters, casting freckles of light in our faces. Again, it was calming and hard but in a good way.

41

The hills I completed made me confident and ready for the next, instead of tired and wanting to take a break. The last chunk before lunch, we were granted access onto a private road that took a long stretch into rich, hunter green spread canyons that ended in rocky drops. The whole road there was either flat or slightly downhill, so we literally didn't work for an hour and a half at least. Actually the best.

Also, at one point we rode past this mini waterfall trickling droplets of Maya blue that caught the light as it cascaded downward, creating a shining-crystal effect. It was tucked in a tree nook at a turn, and dropping trees had rooted themselves (literally) on the side of the rocky walls to cast overhang shadows that shaded the waterfall and supplied even more dimension.

Then we stopped at the library for lunch, which wasn't sandwiches (I know, I surprised you there)—it was tacos! There was this sticky note thing in the actual library (because I forgot to mention we had lunch in a big room *next* to the library—never eat around books, kids) that Jessia and I organized. I also read chapters of *Keeper of the Lost Cities Exile* because I was bored, and it's one of my favorite series. I have read Percy Jackson, Harry Potter, the whole shabang, and *Keeper of the Lost Cities* is still better. I'm not sorry.

I just chilled until we left. It was ups and downs, and was fun with Jessica at my side. Then we had to walk a ways to camp because of traffic.

Jessica, Coral, and I were playing with slime in the RV, and it was funny because Jessica took some of her mom's pie slice. That doesn't sound funny but it was. Then Coral, Dad,

Coral's grandparents, Kelly, Carter (Coral's brother), Eric, and I went to Red Robin at the mall, and Coral and I got a Cinnabun to split in the morning (Jessica and her mom went to their house that night). Camp was the Archaeological Center in Escondido.

Then we drove home, and Coral and I went to the campfire. It was emotional because tomorrow is the last day. It's just something you get used to-the rides every weekend, running errands to look for supplies, even the one week became routine. And one I was going to miss. For the last story, I was expecting a bang to end the series, but was rather told one not as suspenseful as I had been anticipating, just about the history and speculations of the graveyard we were sleeping beside. Now I'm writing.

P.S. Coral and Carter were so funny together. Just the

way they talk/argue. Oh, it was super hard not to laugh. I know at the beginning I said I just wanted RAC to end, but now I just want it to last forever. Sometimes you don't know what you have until it's gone.

Anyways, goodnight. I don't really know what to say. Life is a curious thing. BAWAAAH! Sorry, I just burst out laughing about how cheesy and weird that sounded. I just meant everything's cool and weird, you know? Like how will we ever know how many universes there are, or if time is an illusion, or if there's multiple dimensions and duplicates of everyone, or how our world even started? Ok, I'm getting off track, goodnight.

*I just thought it was funny because I had it as "dancing" and it kept trying to tell me to change it to "dancin,'" so I did.

Day Seven

ARCHEOLOGICAL CENTER TO MOONLIGHT BEACH

April 14, 2018

I'm writing this Sunday because I was too tired to do it last night. This morning I didn't really want to wake up. So it took me a while to get up.

Apparently Coral had to go home because something happened with their RV (or, I don't know), but upon hearing this, I had cereal (if you were curious, Cheerios and Frosted

Flakes). Yeah. Oh, our tent was right next to Soraya, picnic tables, and the cemetery. I got ready and stuff, then Coral came and gave me the Cinnabun. Oh, by the way, you may think me insane (or not, I don't know), but this was my first time having one, and it was pretty good. Not amazing, but not terrible either.

My dad and I rode with Soraya and her dad, and I left really nervous, excited, and sad. I was excited for the really good apple pie at the beach Jessica had been talking about. Christiane said there'd be no hills, but that was a bit far from the truth. Almost right away, there was this gradual hill that was so long, it seemed endless. Then we rode on through, like, a forest, and it was really pretty, but there were some really hard hills. Finally we got to the rest stop, which was a park. The park had a pretty fountain and a cafe across from it, and Dad took me there. I got cheesy scrambled eggs with potatoes, toast, and fruit, which filled me up nicely.

Then we went back, and I found Coral and Jessica sitting on a wall, so I sat with them. Then we went to the bathroom with Mrs. Leibowitz and, when we were walking, I learned that the makeup ride was on the weekend of encampment we were hosting, so I wouldn't be doing that. Even though I'd already decided I was doing it, that was a huge weight off my shoulders. But I was still kinda sad because I wanted to do it. I mean, it was only fifteen miles.

We headed back and took pictures. That took forever trying to organize everybody, and the glaring sun didn't help, but I think the finished product turned out pretty well. I also got a picture with Denis. Apparently this girl was walking on the edge of the fountain and slipped and fell in the foundation and hurt her ankle. Also on Thursday, only a mile from camp, this girl Emma fell, chipped her tooth, and now has a sprain on one arm and a cast on the other. I felt really bad for both of them. Then we left, but Soraya and I left late because we were trying to find someone's sunglasses-I don't remember whose-right as we were trying to leave.

Then there were some hills but also really nice down-hills. Eventually, we made it to this grassy area where the parents would go first to take pictures. The girl who fell also fortunately rode those parts. I caught up with Jessica and Coral, and we made it to the middle-ish. We had a mile until the beach! At the last part, you went down a hill onto this dead end where cars turned around. All along the turnaround, people were cheering and holding signs, and you rode through them to the sand. I couldn't help but smile, and I even saw Mrs. Regardie (my teacher!) plus her daughters, Elizabeth and Juliette. My mom and Gavin found us, and we went to go dip our tires in the ocean. Then we hung around, talked a bit, and headed home. I had been hit with what I thought was a unique idea, and that was to search for a rock to keep as a memento from the trip, as I would only be at this beach at the end of RAC once. I didn't have a collection or anything, so really any rock would do. Unfortunately, I was caught up in all the celebrations that I totally spaced and forgot!

By the time we left the beach, it was 3:50, and Gordon's party was at four o'clock, and it took thirty minutes to get home. We got home, and I took a shower. It felt really nice to back home, but unfortunately my lips were really chapped. Oh, I also learned that next weekend I had a camping trip with Girl Scouts. In Julian. What a coincidence. As of right now, I know we're down to eight people because Jessica and Makenzie aren't going. So we'll be able to fit everyone in Mrs. Melissa's tent (my troop leader).

Get this: Jessica's going to Arizona to visit her grandma. She could start RAC, and I could finish it. Cause like, you know, RAC started in Arizona and almost ended in Julian. Then I went to my desk and found a notebook and a gift card to Barnes and Noble, plus a note from my grandparents who watched Gavin because my mom had to work. It was super sweet of them. I also got a little inspiring picture frame from my mom. Then we went to Gordons' party at the "fashionably late" time of 6:15. Only Makenzie and Mckenna were there, so we just talked. The tacos there were amazing, and Makenzie and I watched Lisa and Mckenna play Backgammon. Then after they finished Makenzie and I learned and played it, and it's actually really fun (10/10, would recommend)! Mostly when we talked, I told them about RAC, but Makenzie finished book five of *Keeper of the Lost Cities,* and we talked about that! She admits it's the best series ever. Then I went home and conked out on the bed that felt so much more comfortable after a week on a mat.

It's weird, or at least for me it is, to just write "And that was RAC". It just seems so much more, but also like it was all just a dream and I suddenly woke up, wondering where I am. You get so used to RAC because you've been training for about six months, and the actual thing is a full week, so you just feel weird and empty when it's over. You had to log at least 350 miles and do at least two Escondido rides over such a long stretch, and it ends just like that. In a snap.

At the beginning of RAC I just wanted it to end, but at the end I didn't want it to be over. It's kinda hard to explain, but all I can say is that I'm 100 percent glad I did RAC. I'll never forget it, and I'll consider doing it again. I just don't know, but one thing is for sure: RAC is (hm, how to end this in a way you won't forget) . . . nice . . .? RAC finished. For the twenty-eighth year . . .

Aftermath

April 15, 2018

Today was a good day-lying around and relaxing. But tomorrow I have school (blah), and I have a science test on Wednesday. My lips are doing better, thanks to the bucket of Vaseline in the medicine cabinet that I have no recollection ever buying. I also started watching Tasty after Soraya showed it to me, and it's cool.

It was actually really nice because it ended up being that Mrs. Regardie let all the kids who did RAC just kinda chill. Shoutout to her, she's the best. Oh, also, I want to tell Mckenna about this sign I saw that had a sticker that said "eating animals" right under the "stop" on a stop sign. I think I'll make smoothies in the morning. Goodnight, I'm getting tired. It's been one day, only one, but it feels so strange not riding or thinking about riding. I'm gonna miss RAC training rides. But I'm gonna have a lot of free time. Also my camping trip is this weekend, which I'm excited for.

Reunion

? (I'm sorry I have no idea, I will tell you if I figure it out)
Sometime before May 20, 2018 and after April 15, 2018

S o let me explain the reunion before I continue because you are probably confused and demanding answers. By the way, this is going to be a short entry because I don't remember too many small details, but I definitely have the big picture and I wanted to recount anything that has to do with RAC. Anyways, the reunion is literally just a potluck where all the people from RAC that year get together again for old time's sake. Fifth graders also receive their award and can share something in front of the crowd. (And my book is born. Kinda.) Long story short, the food was good, I played with people, and then we went into the auditorium.

I forgot to mention that this was at Sundance Elementary, and it reminded me of that time I walked into my neighbor's house and saw what would've been if you put my house in front of a mirror. Major deja vu. So I shared one day of my journal (the second day, if you were wondering) and also listened to other people tell their stories. Then we watched a video of a bunch of pictures and got our awards as well as sang a homemade song about RAC. So yeah. The end. (What else am I supposed to put for the ending? Annyeonghaseyo? (According to Google, that's Korean for "goodbye".)

RAC Makeup Ride

May 20, 2018

After the Reunion

Today was the RAC makeup for Thursday, and, not going to lie, pretty trying. It might have been because it'd been awhile since I'd been rigorously training, or that it was one, if not the most, strenuous day of the week. Some would say that's because of Banner Grade, the gradual but endless hill that lasts approximately six miles, and others would continue with Killer Hill, among others. I woke up at 6:00, but I was running Girl Scout Brownie Encampment, so I had to leave early. There was this really sweet Brownie there, and her name was also Kaelyn (I don't know how you spell her name but for convenience I'm spelling it differently than my own). She was super sweet, and I was sad I had to leave early. My dad picked me up, and I had a chocolate muffin and a banana for breakfast. We drove with Dean and Travis (two people we met on RAC, Dean being the father, Travis the son). When Dad asked Travis if he'd ridden his bike since RAC and Travis said no,

Dean responded with, 'Lazy bum." It was hilarious. We were getting ready to start, and I was so nervous. This was the one day that had the hills everyone most dreaded. I found Maddie, and we rode with her. Gorilla Hill looked near impossible when we shuttled, and unfortunately no hurricane had come along and blown it up while I was gone. Gah, it was challenging. A nibble of what was to come. Finally I made it and we kept going until the regroup.

Maddie gave me some waffle thing and an energy gummy, and they were really good. We were at the front, but then Dad had a flat tire and then we had to wait and ended up last. And we were off like a herd of turtles. Maddie was fast, so she went and sped ahead. Dad wasn't feeling well, so he fell behind. It was just me and Mindy, Maddie's mom. It was Banner Grade time, and there was a huge white "B" on a side mountain for Banner and a "K" for Killer Hill. *Doesn't that just sound so fun?* By the way, we started at Stagecoach, the little shop that we had regrouped and shuttled.

I don't think I could have done Banner without Mindy. She was seriously so helpful. Before she came to my rescue, I was struggling and going slow, but she guided me in when exactly to shift. This hill was six or seven miles, and I didn't stop once! I felt so bad that we left my dad, but I didn't want to break my cadence. I can't describe how well it felt riding again! The canyons were also beautiful, and bursting with flourishing trees and shrubs that glowed with sunlight. Finally, we made it up Banner Grade, and received our apple pie. I waited for my dad and saw him come in.

Maddie-again-gave us those delicious citrus gummies. We only had 3.2 miles left!

When we started it was going smoothly, but Mindy got a flat on a hill. Maddie and I couldn't stop on a hill, so we persevered and flew through the remainder of the make-up. There were like two hard hills, some down, and uneventful flat roads. A mix of everything. Today was a total of eighteen miles. Speeding down the hills was pretty fun, the wind blowing our hair away from our reddened cheeks. Then we go to the pizza place just in front of our parents. Sadly, we couldn't have pizza because we had to go to make it to Makenzie's birthday party, which is exactly where we headed after we finished.

We were forty-five minutes late, so I didn't get to shower, but oh well. We just chilled at Makenzie's and had pizza, ice cream, and cake. We played volleyball and watched the *Greatest Showman* (now one of my favorites!). Now I'm home. Took a refreshing shower. I'm also kinda sunburned, and unbearably sore. And definitely dreading the math test we have tomorrow.

I'm so glad I had the opportunity to finish today. In my eyes, I couldn't give myself full credit without finishing every mile. I also just longed for the push of my feet against the pedals, my hands gripping the handlebars, the wind cooling my cheeks. It's just cool to have this, as many people don't have the resources I'm grateful to have, and it'll for sure be something I'll reference from time to time with a smile, recalling my incredible hardships and victories.

Conclusion

January 4, 2019 at like two in the morning
(I'm just messing with you, it's 11:35 in the morning.)

To future generations, I say, "Just do it!" Sign up. You can back out (I think, I don't know, don't take my word), or you can break your arm and *have* to back out. What I'm saying is, you only get one chance. One. I would take advantage. And, hey, you can at least say you did it! How many people get to do that?

Look at me. I loved it so much, I'm doing it again. And if you remember, before RAC I sucked at riding, even *hated* it. So much has changed.

Yes, I did describe hard parts, but that's just me complaining. It felt good to accomplish them and even better to ride the easy parts (which do exist!). If you are really having a hard time convincing yourself, have someone do it, like your friend. Or convince your friend. Even better!

Just promise me to consider it. Actually consider, too; don't follow in my footsteps and say, "It's too hard—nope."

My friend tells me how glad she is that she didn't do

RAC, but all I can think of when she says that is all that she missed out on. The amazing bonds you create with people. The late-night campfires with history, stories, pep talks. The people cheering you on as you complete the end of the ride. Just simply laughing with your friends in an RV about nothing important.

Please. Don't make the mistake I almost did!

Just do it.

About the Author

Kailyn Donnelly is thirteen and in seventh grade. She loves the color grey and dandelions. She also enjoys reading, laughing, and wearing her favorite T-shirts. Her favorite season is fall, while her favorite subject is math. She lives in San Diego with her mom, dad, younger brother, and dog.

Kailyn's favorite hobby is playing volleyball at San Diego Volleyball Club. She also does Girl Scouts and confirmation. She likes writing because you can write about whatever strikes your fancy, and however you want. She decided to turn her RAC journal into a published book because being an author is a career she is considering, and thought it would be a fun challenge while learning more about the publication process.

To contact Kailyn, please email donnelly.racjournal@gmail.com

If you're inspired to participate in the RAC ride after reading Kailyn's story, please visit https://www.rideacrosscalifornia.com/ to learn more about training and bike requirements, code of conduct, and more!

Made in the USA
Las Vegas, NV
16 February 2021